D1606855

ATTACK VEHICLES IN THE AIR
FIGHTERS AND BOMBERS

by Craig Boutland

CAPSTONE PRESS
a capstone imprint

Edge Books are published by Capstone Press,
1710 Roe Crest Drive, North Mankato, Minnesota 56003
www.mycapstone.com

Published in 2020 by Capstone Publishing Ltd

Library of Congress Cataloging-in-Publication Data
Cataloging-in-publication information is on file with the Library of Congress.

ISBN: 978-1-5435-7379-4 (library binding)
ISBN: 978-1-5435-7386-2 (eBook PDF)

For Brown Bear Books Ltd:
Editorial Director: Lindsey Lowe
Design Manager: Keith Davis
Children's Publisher: Anne O'Daly
Picture Manager: Sophie Mortimer

Photo Credits
Front Cover: Shutterstock: Everett Historical
Interior: Alamy: 508 Collection, 4-5, Flight Plan 18-19; iStock: VanderWolf Images, 26-27, 27tr; Ministry of Defence
UK, Corporal Mike Jones, 29t; Public Domain: Mohamoud Bali, 7tr, Senior Airman Ricky Best, 19br, US Airforce/
arcweb.archives.gov, 6, Alan Wilson/Cambs Uk, 16bl; Shutterstock: Fasttailwind, 20-21, IanC66, 14bl, 14-15,
InsectWorld, 24-25, Shuravi07, 28tr, Joseph Sohm, 7tl, Sam Whitfield1, 24bl; US Department of Defense: 20bl,
US Airforce, 7b, 8bl, 8-9, 10bl, 12bl, 12-13, 16-17, 28bl, 29c, US Airforce/photo by Senior Airman Gustav Gonzalez,
22bl, 22-23, US Navy, 29b.

Brown Bear Books has made every attempt to contact the copyright holders.
If you have any information please contact licensing@brownbearbooks.co.uk

Printed in China.
1671

TABLE OF CONTENTS

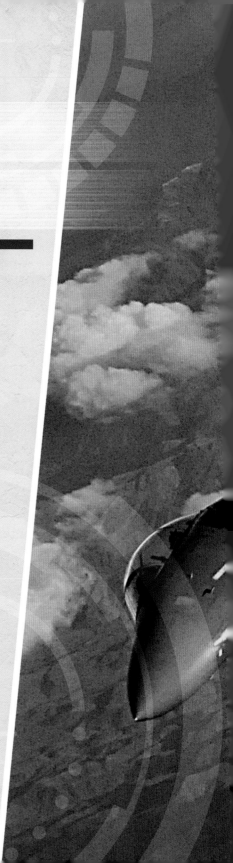

FIGHTERS AND BOMBERS

The war on terrorism was launched by the United States in 2001. It was a response to the September 11th attacks on the World Trade Center and the Pentagon. Although it is a global war, most military action takes place in Afghanistan, Pakistan, and Iraq.

Attack aircraft fight the enemy from the air. They use **smart munitions** or swoop low and release their weapons directly. Attack aircraft seek and destroy targets on land or at sea. Many attack aircraft can also fight enemy planes in the air.

Much of the air war on terrorism takes place in mountainous regions and deserts. Attack aircraft must be fast, easy to control, and be able to withstand temperature shifts and missile attacks from enemies on the ground.

smart munitions—electronically controlled weapons that can detect, locate, and destroy specific targets

An F-15E Strike Eagle drops flares over Afghanistan in 2008.

TIMELINE OF THE WAR ON TERRORISM

September 2001
Terrorists from a group called al-Qaeda, led by Osama bin Laden, capture four U.S. commercial airliners. Two of the airplanes are flown into the twin towers of the World Trade Center in New York City. The Pentagon in Washington, D.C. is also attacked. The fourth plane crash lands in Pennsylvania. In total, 2,996 people die.

February 2006
Al-Qaeda bombs the Shia al-Askari Mosque in Iraq. This is part of widespread violence between Sunni and Shia Muslims in Iraq. Tens of thousands of people die.

2001 — **2003** — **2006** — **2011**

October–November 2001
U.S. forces and their **coalition allies** invade Afghanistan, where al-Qaeda was based. Afghanistan is run by the Taliban, an extreme Islamic political group. Coalition forces quickly overrun the country. They capture the capital, Kabul, in November. The Taliban go into hiding and continue the war.

March–December 2003
U.S. and coalition forces invade Iraq. They capture the capital, Baghdad, in April. In December, Iraqi president Saddam Hussein is captured. Islamic extremists and other groups fight on against the coalition forces.

May 2011
A U.S. Navy SEAL team locates and kills Osama bin Laden in Pakistan, where he had been in hiding.

December 2014
U.S. President Barack Obama announces the end of the U.S. combat role in Afghanistan. Afghan government forces take over all combat duties as the war against the forces of the Taliban continues.

January 2015
ISIS (a terrorist group sometimes called Islamic State) splits away from al-Qaeda. ISIS takes control of the city of Fallujah in Iraq.

October 2017
ISIS loses control of Raqqa, its last major stronghold in Iraq. It has also been forced to withdraw from major towns in Syria. From October 2014 to 2017, U.S. forces launched more than 20,000 air strikes against ISIS in Iraq and Syria.

2014 **2015** **2017**

April 2014
The Boko Haram Islamic extremist group in Nigeria kidnaps 276 female school students. In 2018, 112 of them were still missing.

December 2015
ISIS takes control of large areas of Iraq and Syria. It enforces strict Islamic laws that set out how Muslims should lead their lives. "Operation Inherent Resolve" is launched against ISIS by U.S. attack aircraft.

June 2018
The Afghan government and the Taliban announce a ceasefire for the Eid holiday that ends Ramadan.

coalition allies—members of a group of people or countries working together toward a common goal

7

F-16 FIGHTING FALCON

The F-16 Fighting Falcon is also called the "Viper." It went into service in 1978. The Viper is easy to steer and is used by U.S. forces in air-to-ground combat against terrorists in Afghanistan and Iraq.

IN ACTION

A maintenance crew removes the huge engine from an F-16 Fighting Falcon at Bagram Air Field, in Afghanistan, in 2014. The engine was scheduled for an overhaul.

RESCUE

0436

VULCAN cannon is fixed in the upper left side of the **fuselage**.

ALUMINUM SHEETS cover 80 percent of the F-16's body.

WEIGHT: 25,500 pounds (12,000 kilograms) loaded

LENGTH: 50 feet (15 meters)

TOP SPEED: 1,320 miles (2,120 kilometers) per hour

CREW: one

MAIN WEAPONS one 20 mm Vulcan cannon, air-to-air and air-to-ground missiles, rockets

EXTERNAL MISSILES are fixed under the wings and on the wingtips.

fuselage—the main body of an aircraft

F-35A LIGHTNING II

The F-35A Lightning II is an advanced stealth fighter that first went into action in 2018. Its design and speed make it hard for enemy aircraft to track.

IN ACTION

The F-35A **stealth** aircraft identifies and strikes targets in the air and on the ground. The U.S. Air Force also uses F-35As to track and observe enemy movements.

A **HELMET MOUNTED DISPLAY SYSTEM** (HMDS) projects data onto the pilot's visor.

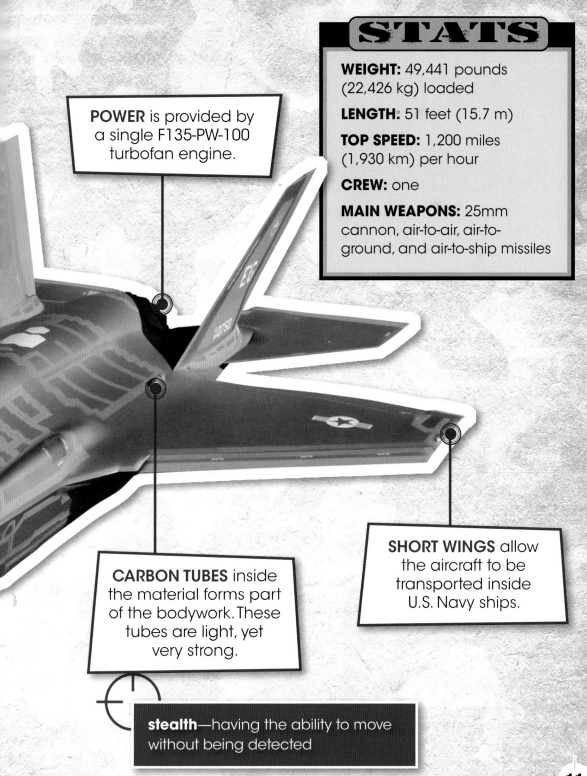

POWER is provided by a single F135-PW-100 turbofan engine.

STATS

WEIGHT: 49,441 pounds (22,426 kg) loaded

LENGTH: 51 feet (15.7 m)

TOP SPEED: 1,200 miles (1,930 km) per hour

CREW: one

MAIN WEAPONS: 25mm cannon, air-to-air, air-to-ground, and air-to-ship missiles

CARBON TUBES inside the material forms part of the bodywork. These tubes are light, yet very strong.

SHORT WINGS allow the aircraft to be transported inside U.S. Navy ships.

stealth—having the ability to move without being detected

B-2A SPIRIT

The B-2A is sometimes called the "flying wing" because of its shape. It is a heavy bomber. It can fly long distances without needing to land to refuel.

IN ACTION

B-2As can be refuelled in the air. They have flown to Afghanistan, dropped bombs, and flown back to U.S. air bases without stopping.

THE AIRCRAFT is painted with a **radar**-absorbent coating. This makes it hard for enemy radar to detect the aircraft.

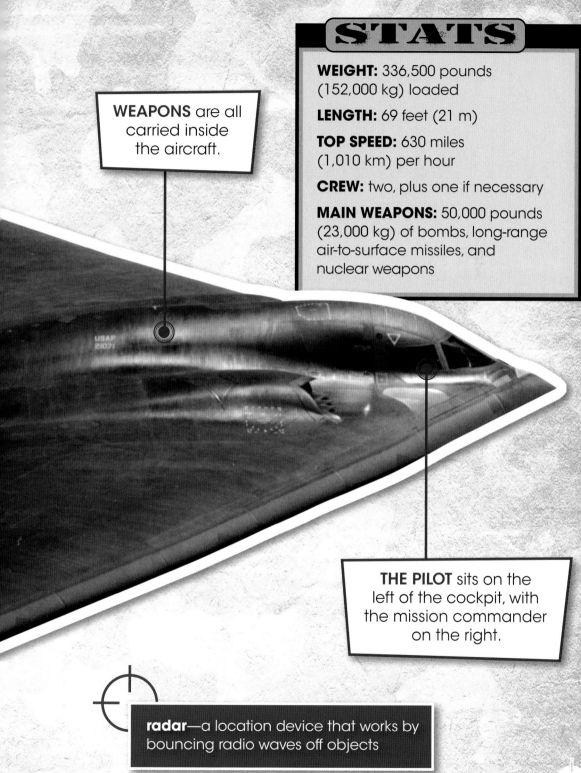

WEAPONS are all carried inside the aircraft.

WEIGHT: 336,500 pounds (152,000 kg) loaded

LENGTH: 69 feet (21 m)

TOP SPEED: 630 miles (1,010 km) per hour

CREW: two, plus one if necessary

MAIN WEAPONS: 50,000 pounds (23,000 kg) of bombs, long-range air-to-surface missiles, and nuclear weapons

THE PILOT sits on the left of the cockpit, with the mission commander on the right.

radar—a location device that works by bouncing radio waves off objects

B-52H STRATOFORTRESS

B-52H Stratofortresses are large, long-range bombers that can be refuelled in flight. They can fly at low altitudes and carry up to 30 bombs. They have been used extensively by the U.S. Air Force in Afghanistan and Iraq.

IN ACTION

The B-52H had a crew of 6 until the 1990s, when the tail guns were removed from all B-52Hs. The rear gunner was no longer needed.

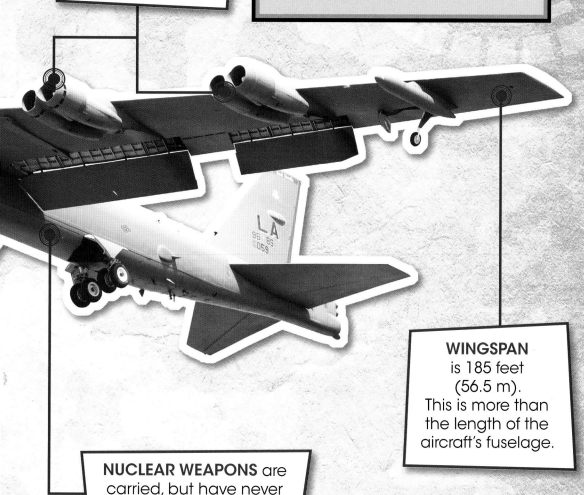

POWER is provided by eight engines mounted in four double pods. There are two double pods on each wing.

NUCLEAR WEAPONS are carried, but have never been dropped in combat.

WINGSPAN is 185 feet (56.5 m). This is more than the length of the aircraft's fuselage.

B-1B LANCER

B-1B Lancers are heavy bombers that provide long-range strike power for the U.S. Air Force. The Lancer can fly at altitudes of up to 60,000 feet (18,000 m).

LOW CROSS-SECTION BODY PROFILE makes the B-1B Lancer hard for enemy radar to detect.

IN ACTION

In the Iraq War (2003-2011), B-1B Lancers flew less than one percent of the coalition combat missions but dropped 43 percent of the smart munitions used.

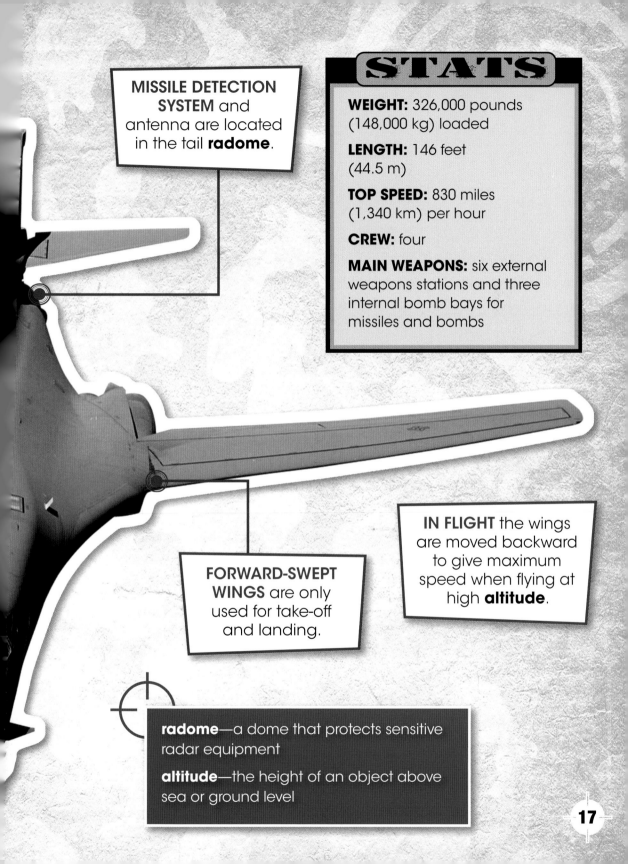

MISSILE DETECTION SYSTEM and antenna are located in the tail **radome**.

STATS

WEIGHT: 326,000 pounds (148,000 kg) loaded

LENGTH: 146 feet (44.5 m)

TOP SPEED: 830 miles (1,340 km) per hour

CREW: four

MAIN WEAPONS: six external weapons stations and three internal bomb bays for missiles and bombs

IN FLIGHT the wings are moved backward to give maximum speed when flying at high **altitude**.

FORWARD-SWEPT WINGS are only used for take-off and landing.

radome—a dome that protects sensitive radar equipment

altitude—the height of an object above sea or ground level

17

E-8C JOINT STARS

The E-8C Joint Surveillance Target Attack Radar System (STARS) is a flying mission control room for U.S. forces in action. The aircraft has played a key role in tracking down terrorists in Iraq and Afghanistan.

GA
50042

WORKSTATIONS inside the aircraft provide a wide range of computer software for use in action.

TURBOFAN ENGINES power the aircraft.

WEIGHT: 336,000 pounds (152,407 kg) loaded

LENGTH: 153 feet (47 m)

TOP SPEED: 587 miles (945 km) per hour

CREW: four flight crew, up to 18 specialist crew

EQUIPMENT: radar and computerized tracking systems

600 TARGETS can be tracked at any one time at a distance of up to 150 miles. (250 km).

IN ACTION

The E-8C STARS tracks individual vehicles or small groups of **insurgents** on the ground. It interacts with U.S. Army base stations and directs other airforce units to the terrorists' location.

insurgent—a person fighting against his or her own government or an invading force

F-15E STRIKE EAGLE

F-15E Strike Eagles are deadly attack aircraft. They are quick and able to fly at low altitudes. Strike Eagles support **ground troops** in Afghanistan by locating and destroying enemy positions.

IN ACTION

F-15Es have been engaged in most of the wars that the U.S. has fought since 1990. In Afghanistan, F-15Es stayed airborne for up to 15 hours at a time, refuelling 12 times.

THE COCKPIT is equipped with computer screens, radar, infrared sensors, moving map displays, and other technology.

RADAR can pinpoint targets up to 10 miles (16 km) away.

STATS

WEIGHT: 81,000 pounds (36,700 kg) loaded

LENGTH: 64 feet (19.5 m)

TOP SPEED: 1,875 miles (3,017 km) per hour

CREW: one pilot and one weapons systems officer

MAIN WEAPONS: one 20mm cannon, 23,000 pounds (10,400 kg) of bombs or missiles

EXTERNAL FUEL TANKS increase the possible range of the aircraft.

ground troops—soldiers who fight on the ground, rather than at sea or in the air

F-22 RAPTOR

The F-22 Raptor carries a large number of weapons, including bombs and missiles. Its top speed is more than twice the speed of sound. The design of the aircraft makes it harder for enemy radar to track it.

IN ACTION

The cockpit has digital flight instruments. The pilot reads information on six LCD panels. They present information in full color and are readable in direct sunlight.

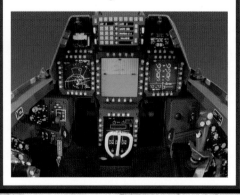

INTERNAL WEAPONS BAYS reduce external **air resistance**.

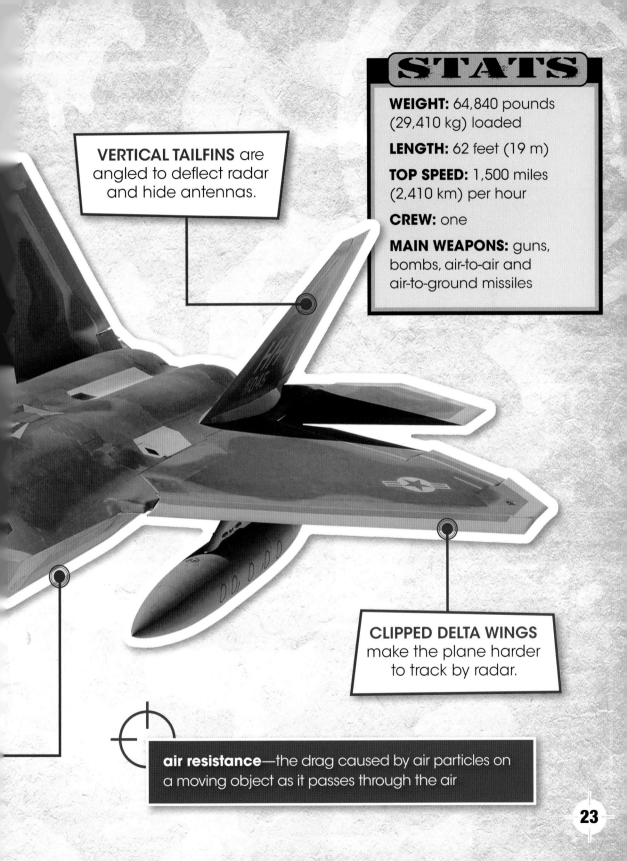

VERTICAL TAILFINS are angled to deflect radar and hide antennas.

CLIPPED DELTA WINGS make the plane harder to track by radar.

air resistance—the drag caused by air particles on a moving object as it passes through the air

EUROFIGHTER TYPHOON

The Eurofighter Typhoon jet fighter was designed to fight enemy aircraft. It carries bombs and missiles. Countries using the Eurofighter include Britain, Spain, Italy, and Germany.

TAIL WING displays the tail badge of the British Royal Air Force 11th Squadron.

IN ACTION

Eurofighter Typhoons have been used in Iraq and Syria. In 2016, Royal Air Force Typhoons made use of their **precision-guided** bombs. They helped coalition forces to advance through Hajin to attack ISIS groups in Syria.

STATS

WEIGHT: 35,270 pounds (16,000 kg) loaded

LENGTH: 52 feet (16 m)

TOP SPEED: 1,550 miles (2,495 km) per hour

CREW: one

MAIN WEAPONS: one 27mm Mauser cannon, 19,800 pounds (9,000 kg) of bombs and missiles

THE PILOT wears a special helmet that displays information on a screen in front of his or her eyes.

EXTERIOR WEAPONS STATIONS known also as hardpoints, allow the Typhoon to carry extra weapons. The Typhoon has 13 hardpoints.

precision-guided—describes bombs or missiles that are designed to lock onto and hit targets with great accuracy

MIRAGE 2000D

The Mirage 2000D is an air-to-ground attack aircraft. It is the main strike airplane of the French Air Force and carries laser-guided nuclear weapons. The Mirage has been **deployed** to attack and destroy terrorist groups in Iraq.

STATS

WEIGHT: 23,550 pounds (10,680 kg) loaded

LENGTH: 48 feet (14.55 m)

TOP SPEED: 1,453 miles (2,338 km) per hour

CREW: two

MAIN WEAPONS: rockets, missiles, bombs, and laser-guided nuclear weapons

ONE TURBOFAN ENGINE is mounted on the fuselage. A large single exhaust sticks out past the tail.

IN ACTION

The Mirage 2000D can be refuelled while it is in the air. This Mirage is receiving fuel from a U.S. Air Force tanker while in the air over Iraq in April 2016.

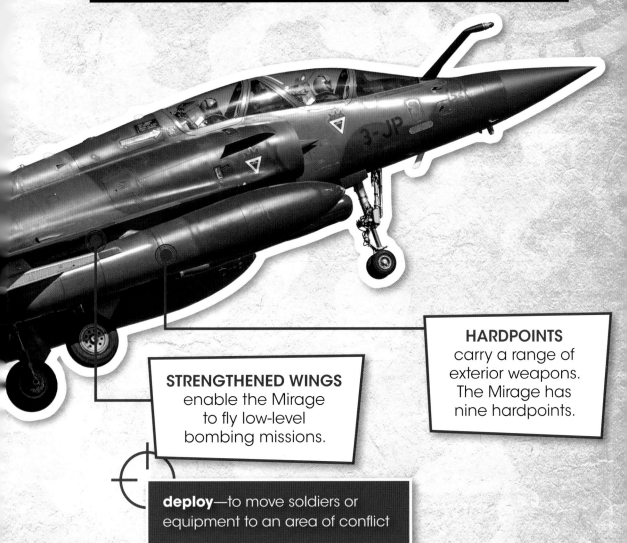

STRENGTHENED WINGS enable the Mirage to fly low-level bombing missions.

HARDPOINTS carry a range of exterior weapons. The Mirage has nine hardpoints.

deploy—to move soldiers or equipment to an area of conflict

OTHER AIRCRAFT

Other aircraft have also flown into action against terrorist groups. These aircraft play a number of different roles. They have mainly been used to defend ground troops from enemy attack.

Sukhoi Su-25

The U.S. Thunderbolt's major weapon is a 7-barrel 30 mm cannon. The Thunderbolt is protected with more than 1,200 pounds (540 kg) of titanium armor.

A-10 Thunderbolt

The Su-25 is a Russian **close-air support** aircraft. It has been used in Syria to attack terrorists. The Su-25 has a long combat history. It has been in service for 30 years.

This aircraft is used by the British Royal Air Force and other European countries. It has been used in conflicts in Iraq, Afghanistan, and Syria since 2001. In September 2014 a pair of Tornados attacked an ISIS heavy weapons base.

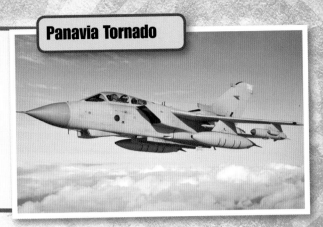

Panavia Tornado

A-29 Super Turcano

The Super Turcano was developed in Brazil. It is a small, propeller-driven attack aircraft. It has been particularly effective in Afghanistan, where it can fly at low speeds and low altitudes in extreme heat.

The Hornet is a U.S. Navy plane used for air-to-air operations. In 2003, Hornets were used during attack operations in Iraq. They flew from bases within the country, and also from carriers off the coast.

A/F-18 Hornet

close-air support—an aircraft that helps to protect or support troops fighting on the ground in war zones

GLOSSARY

air resistance (AYR-ri-ZISS-tuhnss)—the drag caused by air particles on a moving object as it passes through the air

altitude (AL-i-tood)—the height of an object above sea or ground level

close-air support (KLOHS-ayr suh-PORT)—air action by an aircraft against enemy targets that are located close to friendly forces.

coalition allies (koh-uh-LISH-uhn AL-eyes)—members of a group of people or countries working together toward a common goal

deploy (di-PLOY)—to move soldiers or equipment to an area of conflict

fuselage (FYOOZ-suh-lahzh)—the main body of an aircraft

ground troops (GROUND TROOPS)—soldiers who fight on the ground, rather than at sea or in the air

insurgent (in-SUR-juhnt)—a person fighting against a government or invading force

precision-guided (PRESS-shun-GYDED)—describes bombs or missiles that are designed to lock onto and hit targets with great accuracy

radar (RAY-dar)—a location device that works by bouncing radio waves off objects

radome (RAY-dohm)—a dome that protects sensitive radar equipment

smart munitions (SMART myoo-NI-shuhns)—electronically controlled weapons that can detect, locate, and destroy specific targets

STARS (STARZ)—is the pronounceable word used by the U.S. armed forces that stands for Surveillance Target Attack Radar System

stealth (STELTH)—having the ability to move without being detected

READ MORE

Cooke, Tim. *A Timeline of Fighter Jets and Bomber Planes.* Military Technology Timelines. North Mankato, MN: Capstone Press, 2018.

Hansen, Grace. *Military Attack Aircraft.* Military Aircraft and Vehicles. Minneapolis: Abdo Kids 2017.

Meister, Cari. *Totally Amazing Facts About Military Sea and Air Vehicles.* Mind Benders. North Mankato, MN: Capstone Press, 2017.

Nagelhout, Ryan. *Fighter Planes.* Mighty Military Machines. New York: Gareth Stevens Publishing, 2015.

INTERNET SITES

DK Find Out!
https://www.dkfindout.com/uk/transport/history-aircraft/military-aircraft/

Fighter Planes
https://www.fighter-planes.com/

Jet Fridays
https://duotechservices.com/jet-friday-articles

U.S. Air Force Fact Sheets
https://www.af.mil/About-Us/Fact-Sheets/Indextitle/F/

INDEX